Decoding the love algorithm

What is the truth about relationships and how does any relationship succeed?

Mahmoud Tawfik Selim

Introduction to Relationship Dynamics:

Let's face it, we all crave connection. From the moment we enter this world, our relationships shape us, define us, and impact us in profound ways. But not all connections are created equal. Some relationships enrich our lives, while others drain us dry. The ability to discern between a healthy and a toxic relationship is a skill that can make all the difference in our emotional, mental, and physical well-being.

This book is your comprehensive guide to navigating the treacherous waters of relationship dynamics. Over the following chapters, we will explore the warning signs of unhealthy patterns, the true essence of soul-nourishing connections, and the path to healing from past wounds to build a bright future. But before we dive in, let's establish a foundation by acknowledging the impact of relationships and the objectives of this work.

Relationships and Well-Being

The quality of our close relationships is directly linked to numerous indicators of well-being. Positive social connections foster greater life satisfaction, resilience during hardships, and even longevity. On the flip side, conflictual or abusive ties can be major sources of chronic stress, leading to depression, anxiety, and physical health problems over the long term.

Our early experiences with our parents' marriage or primary caregiver relationships in childhood also leave an indelible mark. These relationships shape how we view ourselves and expect to be treated in future bonds. Children in nurturing, stable homes tend to have higher self-esteem and healthier relationships later on. However, those who grew up amid violence or neglect face an uphill battle to unwind these deep-rooted effects.

Defining Healthy and Unhealthy Dynamics

At their core, healthy relationships involve mutual care, respect, trust, and growth for all parties. Partners in truly happy, balanced couplings report feeling loved, accepted, and supported exactly as they are. Communication flows freely, and conflicts are resolved constructively through compromise instead of attacks.

Unhealthy patterns, in contrast, revolve around control, fear, and instability. Partners may feel unheard, judged, or obliged to stifle their needs to appease volatile counterparts. Signs of unhealthy dynamics include emotional unavailability, criticism, possessiveness, withholding affection as punishment, and rigid gender roles. At their worst, abusive ties involve domestic violence or other forms of harm.

Such dynamics leave scars—decreased self-worth from being "loved" conditionally, anxiety about upsetting partners, and reluctance to open up or set limits thereafter. Over time, the effects accumulate until victims accept dysfunction as normal through trauma bonding with their abusers. Relearning healthy behaviors is a long, arduous journey of self-discovery and reparenting oneself with compassion.

Overview of the Book

This resource aims to guide you along every step of understanding, improving, and healing from negative relationship influences. We will delve deeply into recognizing red flags, gaining insight from research, empowering yourself to change patterns, and building fulfilling bonds. While some lessons may feel uncomfortable, reflect on teachings with an open, nonjudgmental spirit.

Are you ready to embark on this empowering journey of self-discovery? The road ahead promises deeper awareness of your needs and strengths, leaving the past behind to embrace a brighter future. Turn the page to continue learning how to identify unhealthy dynamics, prioritize your well-being, and cultivate the relationships you deserve with care, respect, and courage. Your happiness begins now.

Chapter One: Understanding Real Love

In a world dominated by superficial and fleeting communication, many adults struggle to establish warm and fruitful relationships. However, it is crucial to nurture deep connections based on respect, honesty, and mutual trust. This guide aims to provide you with the necessary information and advice to overcome obstacles and reach this type of love.

Defining Real Love:

Real love is that deep relationship based on respect and appreciation for one another's individuality. It transcends superficial aspects like beauty or pleasure and involves understanding and acknowledging the other person's strengths and weaknesses.

Real love enables both parties to feel safe and secure through acceptance and appreciation of each other in their entirety. It strengthens trust and openness between partners, allowing for a strong relationship built on authentic sharing and active listening.

Importance of Real Love:

In an era ruled by fleeting and superficial relationships, real love, which lasts a lifetime, is a relatively rare concept. Nevertheless, it holds immense significance in providing a sense of satisfaction and stability for individuals and society.

Research has shown that deep and enduring relationships contribute to happiness and mental well-being, whereas superficial and temporary relationships are linked to anxiety and mood disorders. Furthermore, real love helps create a strong and well-rounded personality for both individuals, promoting personal and social growth.

Guide Objectives:

This guide aims to help you overcome the obstacles that may hinder the development of deep and lasting relationships.

It will provide you with practical advice and techniques for improving communication skills and self-discovery throughout its chapters. Additionally, you will learn about the leading theories that explain the mechanics of love and relationships.

Topics covered include the importance of self-love, overcoming insecurities, effective communication, and healing from past emotional wounds. All of this aims to help you discover yourself, achieve emotional and psychological balance, and build enduring relationships. Trust in God and never lose hope in the journey of self-discovery and personal growth that will open new horizons in your life.

Conclusion:

This guide aims to equip you with the information and tools necessary to build deep, respectful relationships based on mutual trust. Through it, you will understand the importance of personal growth and self-love in establishing sustainable relationships. Trust in God and never lose hope in the journey of self-discovery that will open new horizons in your life.

Chapter Two:
Understanding Yourself

The Concept of Self :

The concept of self or self-image is a critical component in building healthy relationships. Through an awareness of your strengths and weaknesses, you can understand yourself, and identify your needs and desires in a relationship.

The journey of self-discovery begins in childhood, where the behavior and responses of parents and peers shape your self-image. Children who feel loved and accepted by those around them develop a positive self-concept.

Conversely, those who experience mistreatment or neglect are more prone to low self-esteem or a distorted self-image. Therefore, the journey of self-discovery and acceptance begins in early childhood.

The Theory of Attachment:

John Bowlby's "Attachment Theory" provides a conceptual framework for understanding how relationships are formed. The theory posits that the quality of interaction between parents and children in early childhood affects the development of attachment styles in individuals.

Children who receive sensitive and stable emotional care from their parents develop a secure attachment style. On the other hand, those who face rejection or instability develop defense mechanisms such as wariness or fear of rejection, which reflects in their future relationships.

Attachment Theory explains how childhood interactions influence self-esteem, self-confidence, and communication with others. It is a crucial concept for understanding the dynamics of relationships.

Attachment styles and how they shape adult relationships:

The behaviors displayed in a relationship, particularlywhen the relationship is in danger, define attachment stylesor types. When it comes to relationship issues, a person witha secure attachment type, for instance, might be able to talk about their feelings honestly and ask for help. On the otherhand, those with insecure attachment styles could shy awayfrom intimacy altogether, act selfishly or manipulatively when they're feeling vulnerable, or become needy or clingyin their closest relationships.

You can better understand how you behave, view your partner, and react to intimacy if you are aware of how your attachment style forms and influences your personal interactions. By recognizing these trends, you can better understand what you want from a relationship and how to resolve conflicts.

Ethnicity, culture, wealth, or education are not socioeconomic characteristics that affect the success of attachment. It is also not appropriate to attribute all of your relationship issues to your parent because you have an insecure attachment style as an adult. Your personality as well as events that occurred throughout infancy, adolescence, and adulthood may have influenced the development of your attachment style.

The different attachment styles:

fundamental attachment styles fall into four main categories, each associated with distinct philosophies on intimacy and independence. Gaining awareness of our predominant style sheds light on relationship behaviors while showing the path forward to building healthier bonds.

- *Secure attachment*
- *Anxious (or ambivalent) attachment*
- *Avoidant-dismissive attachment*
- *Disorganized attachment*

1. Secure attachment:

As the base template for relational health, secure attachment arises from consistent and attentive care in childhood. Babies with caregivers who reliably meet basic needs develop a strong sense of self-worth independent of others' approval while also feeling safe depending on loved ones for comfort, guidance, and validation. Into adulthood, securely attached individuals approach intimacy from a balanced perspective. They perceive partners as trustworthy sources of support during difficult times yet feel at ease alone, without deriving identity solely from relationships. Capable of giving and receiving affection freely without losing their sense of autonomy, securely bonded individuals tend to have satisfying long-term relationships and resolve conflicts constructively. They perceive people as generally well-meaning despite inevitable flaws and hold optimistic views of their desirability and ability to influence outcomes. Such resilient confidence stems from internalizing caregiver affection as unconditional rather than something that mustbe constantly earned or justified. Some people might relate to some aspects of stable attachment, but not all of them. You may have particular thought or behavior patterns that trigger arguments with your partner and need to be actively addressed, even if your relationships are generally solid. Start by identifying any similarities you may have with any of the following three types of insecure attachment.

Secure attachment style in relationships:

- *In a close relationship, you can be authentic and see your value, You feel at ease communicating your needs, wants, and hopes.*

- *You enjoy being with other people, you ask your partner for comfort and support without being unduly nervous when you are apart, but you don't get too worried.*

- *You're also pleased that your partner can depend on you for assistance.*

- *In a close relationship, you can keep your emotional equilibrium and look for constructive solutions to resolve disagreements.*

- *You have the fortitude to overcome disappointment, and bad luck in your relationships and other areas of your life.*

2. Anxious (or ambivalent) Attachment:

In contrast, anxious attachment arises from inconsistent care in formative years. Babies faced with unreliable caretakers learn that basic needs may go unmet at any moment, fostering intense fear of abandonment. Eagernessto please and flattery morph into constant vigilance to gauge a partner's shifting moods and retain their engagement. Subconsciously recalling parent-child dynamics where affection depended on perfect behavior, anxiously attached adults struggle to separate their self- worth from others' opinions. Anxious or ambivalent attachment styles, sometimes known as "anxious- preoccupied," "ambivalent- anxious," or just "anxious- ambivalent," are characterized by excessive neediness. As the labels imply, individuals with this attachment style frequently experience anxiety, uncertainty, and low self- esteem. Though they fear rejection from others, they want emotional closeness.

Driven by panic over perceived instability, they exhibit clingy or over-dependent behaviors like excessive reassurance-seeking, emotional outbursts to prevent separation, and merging identities with loved ones at the cost of healthy boundaries. Underlying this overt concern is a fragile sense of self-dooming to find constant validation externally. While desiring intimate bonds, the smothering displayed to maintain proximity ironically distances companions through emotional co-dependence.

Anxious attachment style in relationships:

- *You want closeness and intimacy in a relationship, yet you can't quite trust or be dependent on your partner.*
- *Intimate relationships have a way of taking over your life and making you obsessively focused on the other person.*
- *You can have trouble setting limits because you see the gap between you as a danger that could make you feel*

angry, scared, or afraid that your partner no longer Wants you.

- *You tend to overreact to any perceived dangers to the connection since your sense of self-worth is largely based on how you believe you're being treated in the relationship.*

- *You may use guilt, domineering conduct, or other manipulative strategies to keep your lover close because you feel nervous or envious when they're not around.*

- *You require your companion to provide you with lots of attention and confidence all the time.*

- *You can find it difficult to keep intimate connections going and people might blame you for being overly needy or clinging.*

3. *Avoidant-Dismissive Attachment:*

Alternately, avoidant-dismissive attachment develops from caregiving neglect or rejection in the formative years. Without reliable fulfillment of basic needs for affection and comfort, these children learned suppressing vulnerability proved adaptive for survival. Accustomed to independent problem-solving from a young age, they seem self-sufficientas adults yet harbor profound mistrust in others' availability and consistency. Avoidantly attached individuals prize autonomy to the point of phobia over interdependence and perceive closeness as constraining rather than comforting. Under the guise of independence, they maintain emotional distance and deflect intimacy through distraction techniques or logical justifications for solitude as inherently preferable to disappointment risks. Ironically, the suppressed longing for genuine bonds surfaces erratically as anger, flirtatiousness, or casual relationships lacking depth and commitment. Adults who are ambivalent or anxious-preoccupied are the opposite of those who have an avoidant-dismissive insecure attachment style. Rather than being drawn to proximity, their fear of intimacy makes them want to keep their emotional distance from others. They would prefer not to be dependent on anybody else or to be dependent on others.

Avoidant attachment style in relationships:

- You're a self-sufficient individual who is happy taking care of yourself and doesn't think you need anybody else.

-You tend to retreat more when someone attempts to get close to you or when your partner gets more needy.

- You have trouble expressing your feelings, and others often call you cold, insensitive, inflexible, and intolerant. You accuse them of being too needy in response.

-To reclaim your sense of independence, you often downplay or ignore your partner's emotions, hide details

about them, make secret affairs, and even break up partnerships.

-You could be attracted to partners who are equally self-sufficient and keep an emotional distance from you, or you may prefer temporary, casual relationships over- committed long-term ones.

-We all require intimate relationships and closeness, despite your belief to the contrary. People are by nature social creatures, and even those with avoidant-dismissive attachment styles secretly want a close, meaningful relationship if only they could get over their ingrained phobia of closeness.

4. Disorganized Attachment:

Most complex of all, disorganized attachment results from childhood confusion, threat, abuse, or neglect involving primary caretakers. Faced with the impossible situation of both needing and fearing the very source of care, affected children abandon logical strategies, lashing out or retreating into dissociation. As traumatized adults, disorganized persons oscillate between relationship extremes with explosive anger, volatile anxiety, and unstable self-image fluctuations stemming from unprocessed pain. Relationships feel simultaneously dangerously binding yet

devoid of solace. Core needs remain unreconciled and easily triggered into sudden mood alterations. While yearning for care and control, disabling mistrust impedes bonds based on communication, empathy, and interdependence the very foundations of fulfillment. Without the resolution of past harms through dedicated therapy, an escape from this painful attachment style seems unrealistic. Abuse, neglect, or early trauma are common causes of extreme anxiety that lead to disorganized/disoriented attachment, also known as fearful-avoidant attachment. This type of insecure attachment in adults often makes them believe they are undeserving of affection or intimacy in a relationship.

Disorganized Attachment *style in relationships:*

-You most likely find that close relationships are complex and uncomfortable, frequently shifting between intense feelings of love and hate for a partner.

-Being self-centered, assertive, undependable, and carelessto your partner may end up in unstable or even violent behavior. It is possible to be just as hard on yourself and other people.

-You might use drugs or alcohol, have aggressive or bad behavior patterns, or be violent or aggressive by nature.

- Your failure to accept responsibility for your actions may depress others.

-You feel unworthy of love and afraid of being hurt again, even as you want for the safety and security of a deep, committed relationship.

-It's possible that trauma, abuse, or neglect impacted your childhood.

Let's talk about **Relationship issues:**

stemming from traumatic childhood experiences or past relationships:

-Trust issues and Infidelity: You may question if your partner is being truthful with you about your relationship or other areas of your life.

-Household issues: Arguments over raising kids and doing housework tend to be common.

-Communication issues: If you don't feel heard or understood by your partner, then communication problems could arise.

-Financial issues: A nationwide poll conducted in 2015 by the American Psychological Association (APA) found that one of the main sources of stress in romantic relationships is money.

- *Issues around priorities: Attention and preference issues can lead to relationship troubles, particularly when big decisions need to be made.*

-*Issues around sex and intimacy: Intimacy problems might arise from different sex drives and doubts about attraction and fulfillment.*

-*Life transitions: Relationship setbacks can result from significant life events including menopause, moving, having a baby, and traumatic events.*

-*Violence and abuse: A relationship is most likely abusive if it is characterized by dominance and control. Furthermore, The National Center on Domestic Aggression, Trauma & Mental Health reports thatsubstantial connections have been discovered between drug abuse and aggression against intimate partners.*

Pattern Recognition:

Gaining clarity on the predominant attachment style proves instrumental for personal development yet often proves elusive due to tendencies toward cognitive biases that normalize unhealthy thinking. Systematically reflecting upon past relationship patterns, internal dialogues, and emotional triggers can bring much-needed perspective. While confronting painful realities, recognizing distortions sets the stage for change through acceptance of painful truths previously too frightening to confront. Anxious patterns frequently involve the magnification of potential relationship threats. Always envisioning worst-case scenarios, anxiously attached individuals perceive minor signs of distance like missed calls or delays in text responses as sure signs of disinterest or impending abandonment fueling desperate recoilmeasures.

Consider keeping a journal of automatic thoughts in response to ambiguous partner behaviors like arriving home late from work once without notice. Chances are assumptions veer extreme, like "They must be cheating on me" rather than rationally considering traffic issues. Tracking cognitive distortions reveals beliefs like "If they cared, they would always prioritize me" as falsely elevating intimacy above practical realities. Similarly, relationship patterns often involve compulsive reassurance-seeking or smothering behavior driving loved ones away while confirming core unworthiness beliefs. Past diaries may expose pursuing the same unavailable partner continuously whereas a secure attachment would have accepted "no" with grace. Recognizing this proves half the transformation journey by relinquishing the self-sabotaging stance of blame against others for predictable consequences of dependent behavior.

Avoidantly attached individuals likewise deny distressing emotions through unconscious distortions. While insisting on solitude being "just their style", past notes likely betray subtle signs of loneliness after declining social invitations but lacking the courage to be vulnerable. Consistently invalidating feelings by inventing reasons intimacy seems undesirable or "too much work" serves avoidant defenses rather than acceptance. Unchecked, such distortions prolong isolation despite the profound desire for connection. Discrepancies between insisted self-narratives of happiness alone and physical/ emotional reactions during fleeting social interactions suggest a mandate for honest self-reflection. Rather than berating suppressed needs as "weak", a compassionate lens recognizes their humanity. Disorganized patterns encompass volatile emotional responses implicating unprocessed trauma.Journaling mood fluctuations over time reveals triggers from mundane events suddenly eliciting intense anger, fear, or dissociation without logical cause. Unexplained self-harm tendencies or chaotic romantic choices likelyrelate to unhealed wounds from past harm warranting dedicated support. Overall, identifying biases and inconsistencies between professed beliefs about relationships versus demonstrable behaviors provides an undeniably accurate snapshot of attachment leanings. This fosters empathy toward the vulnerable child within deserves unconditionally loving care rather than self- criticism. Recognizing this represents a giant stride towards crafting patterns encouraging fulfillment and care for inner pain previously too threatening to witness directly. With practice over weeks, meditating upon distortions illuminates conscious or subconscious psychological defenses maintaining the status quo. For example, some anxiously attached individualssubconsciously initiate arguments right before meaningful events to sabotage intimacy as an unconscious panic response rather than a logical decision. By bringing light to darkness and accepting rather than denying difficult realities, transformation becomes attainable. Whereas blaming others or denying problematic behaviors perpetuates suffering, self-awareness releases us from imprisonment within limiting narratives. It affirms self-worth through compassion rather than fragile validation-seeking and empowers the capacity to meet core needs through independence rather than dependence on fluctuating external sources. This forms the bedrock of secure attachments grounded in authenticity rather than fragile constructs threatening to crumble under imagined slights. To supplement introspection, seeking perspectives of trusted friends regarding tendencies not obvious to ourselves proves invaluable for gaining objective insight into relational patterns from September. Examples like canceling plans at the last moment without reason or stonewalling during conflicts bring clarity where *blindspots persist. However, sharing sensitive insights demands a wise selection of confidantes with equal parts empathy and honesty avoiding platitudes favoring existing defenses. Overall, journeying within through attentive self-reflection across time assists in acknowledging the dynamics driving suffering. This fuels deep understanding and compassion crucial to reconstructing secure attachments embracing rather than fearing intimacy, dependence, and independence according to one'sauthentic needs rather than those imposed by childhood circumstances beyond control. Darkness cannot overcome darkness; only light born of truth holds the power to transform.*

Transforming Attachments:

Having gained clarity on predominant insecure attachment leanings through reflection, the next phase centers on practical tools recalibrating thought patterns and developing secure attachment behaviors. While change proves gradual, even small conscious efforts compound significantly over time. Focusing on present responsibilities instead of past hurts allows redirecting energy from unproductive regret into empowering self-care. Mindfulness meditation proves invaluable for dissolving cognitive distortions fueling distress. By non-judgmentally observing thoughts as mental events rather than immutable facts, their emotional charge diminishes. Noticing biases as they arise permits choosing wiser perspectives acknowledging complexity rather than dichotomous extremes. With diligence, this calms excessive anxiety maintaining obsessive reassurance-seeking or anger stemming from purported threats to independence.

Relatedly, emotion regulation skills like deep breathing defuse impulsive reactions perpetuating unhealthy cycles. When distressed, postponing responses using counting or distraction techniques provides perspective minimizing damaging communication. Identifying feelings instead of bottling enables calm processing before addressing concerns respectfully through "I feel" statements avoiding accusations amplifying conflicts. Crucially, developing interests and self-worth independent of relationships guards against codependency and dispels beliefs tying identity to others' opinions. Committing to personal goals, hobbies and self-care like exercise reframes fulfillment as internally rather than externally contingent, increasing resilience when loneliness arises. Daily affirmations counteracting negative self-talk prove profoundly transformational with practice. Authentically communicating needs respectfully while validating a partner's humanity fosters intimacy on equal rather than dependent terms. Clearly outlining boundaries prevents exploiting goodwill or violating autonomy through controlling behaviors rooted in childhood insecurity rather than present realities. Active listening skills like reframing, clarifying, and reflective statements help resolve issues meeting both person necessities. Qualified counseling guides integrating crucial awareness when reflective efforts prove insufficient in resolving entrenched insecurity. Therapists assist in dismantling core maladaptive beliefs through evidence refuting irrational fears. They validate internal strengths resisting discredited viewpoints, improving emotional regulation, and resolving childhood traumas fueling relationship difficulties into adulthood. Committing to this incremental self-directed work demands immense patience, as development cannot be rushed. However, recognizing dysfunctional patterns, educating instincts through knowledge, and exercising compassion towards oneself prove transformative beyond expectations. With diligence, formerly secure attachment behaviors manifest naturally rather than feeling forced, rebuilding self-worth from within independently of external contingencies. Relationships require effort from all parties, yet focusing on improvement inward through awareness, emotional intelligence cultivation, and bolstering self-sufficiency represents the surest path to forming bonds of care, trust, and mutual acceptance of imperfection. Remember - you deserve caring relationships reflecting your authentic needs. Have faith that continued growth moving you nearer to peace and connection, as darkness cannot resist aheart set on loving itself and others. There are always people who can encourage your journey of healing and fulfillment., so keep walking.

The Process of Self-Discovery:

Self-discovery is not limited to childhood but is a lifelong process. There are various techniques to deepen your understanding of yourself over time:

- *Reflecting and listening to your emotions and thoughts.*

- *Keeping a journal to document your experiences and personal reflections.*

- *Engaging in honest conversations with trusted friends who offer a different perspective.*

- *Seeking psychological counseling or behavioral therapy from experts.*

- *Studying personality theories and how they develop and the factors that influence them.*

- *Understanding yourself is essential to personal growth and establishing healthy relationships based on mutual respect and appreciation. So, continue to learn more about yourself.*

To build a fulfilling intimate relationship, it's crucial to balance emotional connection and physical intimacy.

However, before reaching this stage, understanding yourself is key. It involves setting healthy boundaries, communicating your needs and desires, and being open to your partner's feedback.

Chapter Three: Love Yourself
The Fundamental Rule of Relationships

The Concept of Self-Love:

Self-love is defined as the positive feeling of accepting one's self, including acknowledging one's strengths and weaknesses. It is not merely self-absorption or excessive self-esteem, but rather an honest appreciation of one's self, including all the positive aspects.

Achieving Self-Love:

Self-love does not merely come from positive thinking but includes taking actions that reinforce respect for one's self. These include taking care of one's physical and mental health, engaging in hobbies, and actualizing one's potential through work or education.

Importance of Self-Love:

Self-love forms the foundation for building any healthy relationship. A person who does not value themselves will not be able to value others or respond to their needs and desires.

Moreover, a person who doesn't accept their flaws and weaknesses will not be able to accept others' imperfections and shortcomings. Instead, they will be preoccupied with trying to please others instead of taking care of themselves. The significance of self-love becomes apparent when one exudes self-confidence and makes the right decisions. A person who values themselves confidently expresses themselves and stands up for their rights, withouthesitation or vacillation.

Cultivating Self-Love:

There are various practical ways to boost self-love, including:

- *Focusing on strengths and achievements rather than dwelling on flaws.*
- *Avoiding constant comparisons to others and accepting oneself as is.*
- *Respecting personal boundaries and fulfilling one's needs.*
- *Engaging in activities and hobbies that promote self-acceptance.*
- *Distancing oneself from individuals who repeatedly criticize or belittle them.*
- *Expressing achievements and thoughts confidently, rather than hiding them.*

These are just some of the simple steps that can aid in building self-confidence and self-appreciation, which are essential to attaining inner and outer satisfaction.

Conclusion:

Self-love is essential in building healthy and sustainable relationships, as it enables a person to accept themselves and others. Incorporating these easy steps can lead to a greater appreciation of oneself, as well as improved relationships.

Chapter Four: Overcoming Doubt and Fear:
Answers to High Influence and Intimidation

Love, in its purest form, should be a haven of support, trust, and respect. However, sometimes, dynamics within relationships shift, and one partner can find themselves navigating the murky waters of high influence and intimidation.

This chapter will equip you with tools to overcome doubt and fear and reclaim your voice and agency in love.

Understanding the Landscape:

Before diving into solutions, let's identify the red flags of strong influence and intimidation: Constant criticism and belittlement: Your partner undermines your opinions, achievements, and self-worth, chipping away at your confidence.

Who Are Red Flag People?

Red flag people are those charming individuals who, beneath the surface, harbor malevolent intentions. They display toxic behaviors that can wreak havoc on your emotional well-being and relationships. Common traits include a bloated sense of entitlement, lack of accountability, disregard for boundaries, wild moodswings, and attempts to monopolize your time and energy.

Identify The Red Flags:

1. Emotional Red Flags:

Controlling behavior: Possessiveness, constant criticism, attempts to isolate you from friends and family.

Jealousy and distrust: Excessive accusations, unreasonable suspicion, monitoring your activities.

Manipulation and guilt-tripping: Using emotions to coerce you, making you feel responsible for their happiness.

Passive-aggressiveness: *Indirect communication, giving the silent treatment, expressing anger through avoidance.*

Lack of empathy: *Inability to understand or care about your feelings, dismissing your concerns.*

2. Communication Red Flags:

Dishonesty and lying: *Frequent white lies, major deceptions, broken promises.*

Disrespectful communication: *Name-calling, insults, blaming, yelling, interrupting.*

Poor conflict resolution: *Inability to have healthy disagreements, stonewalling, resorting to aggression.*

Closed-mindedness: *Refusal to listen to different perspectives, unwillingness to compromise.*

Unhealthy communication patterns: *Dominating conversations, dismissing your opinions, invalidating your feelings.*

3. Behavioral Red Flags:

Abusive behavior*: Physical, emotional, or verbal abuse, threats, intimidation.*

Addiction issues*: Uncontrolled substance abuse, gambling, or risky behaviors.*

Irresponsible habits*: Financial mismanagement, neglecting commitments, lack of accountability.*

Sudden and extreme changes*: Erratic behavior, mood swings, unpredictable actions.*

Disregard for boundaries*: Disrespecting your personal space, time, and privacy.*

4. Ignoring Your Gut: *The importance of trusting your intuition and recognizing discomfort as a potential sign of something wrong.*

Red flags often escalate over time, and ignoring them can lead to bigger problems later.

Reclaiming Your Power: Remember, you deserve a healthy, respectful relationship.

Here are steps to combat doubt and fear:

Recognize the Patterns: *Acknowledge the presence of these behaviors and their impact on your well-being. Knowledge is power.* **Build Your Support System**: *Confide in trusted friends, family, or a therapist. Sharing your experiences can normalize your feelings and provide invaluable support.*

Set Boundaries: *Clearly communicate your needs and limits. Practice saying "no" and enforcing consequences for unacceptable behavior.*

Gather Information: *Educate yourself on healthy relationships, emotional abuse, and available resources. Knowledge empowers you to make informed decisions.*

Prioritize Your Self-Care: *Engage in activities that nourish your mind, body, and spirit. Reconnect with your passions and strengthen your sense of self.*

Seek Professional Help: If you feel overwhelmed or unsafe, do not hesitate to seek professional support from a therapist or counselor. They can provide personalized guidance and strategies.

Avoid toxic people: *Here are some signs of a toxic person:*

-They are constantly negative and complaining.

-They are manipulative and try to control you. -They take no responsibility for their actions and blame others.

- They put you down and make you feel bad about yourself.

If you have a toxic person in your life, it's important to set boundaries with them or limit your contact with them altogether.

Remember: You are not alone. Many people experience similar challenges in relationships.

Change takes time. Be patient with yourself and celebrate every step towards a healthier dynamic.

You are worthy of respect and love. Never compromise yourself for a relationship that diminishes you.

Moving Forward:

Overcoming doubt and fear is a courageous journey. By recognizing unhealthy patterns, building support, and prioritizing your well-being, you can reclaim your voice and create a love that empowers you, not diminishes you.

you have the strength and resilience to navigate this path, and a fulfilling, respectful relationship awaits on the other side.

Chapter Five:
Skills for Effective
Communication

Cultivating the Language of Love - Skills for Effective Communication:

Love, in its dazzling kaleidoscope of emotions, requires a bridge to flourish truly: effective communication. It's the gentle art of expressing your heart, understanding your partner's, and navigating the beautiful complexities in between. While the journey may not always be smooth, honing these key skills can pave the way for a deeper, more fulfilling connection.

The Art of Listening:

It's often said that we have two ears and one mouth for a reason. Truly listening goes beyond simply hearing words. It's about giving your full attention, both physically and mentally. Put away distractions, maintain eye contact, and nod encouragingly. Show genuine interest by asking clarifying questions and reflecting on what you've heard.

Remember, listening isn't waiting for your turn to speak;

it's creating a safe space for your partner to be heard and understood.

Speaking from the "I":

Instead of accusatory pronouncements like "You never," try "I feel hurt when..." This shift to "I" statements takes ownership of your emotions and avoids placing blame. Express your needs and desires clearly, focusing on solutions rather than dwelling on problems. Be assertive, not aggressive, and remember, respectful communication is always key.

The Power of Empathy: Stepping into your partner's shoes, even when you disagree, fosters a deeper connection. Try to see things from their perspective, acknowledging their feelings without judgment. Validate their experiences, even if you don't always agree. This creates a sense of trust and understanding, the bedrock of any strong relationship.

Finding Common Ground:

Conflict is inevitable, but how you manage it speaks volumes. Focus on the issue at hand, not past grievances. Use "we" statements to emphasize shared goals and avoid getting defensive. Actively listen to each other's concerns, and be open to compromise. Remember, finding solutions requires teamwork, not individual victories.

Celebrate the Everyday:

Communication isn't just about addressing problems; it's about cherishing the good times too. Express appreciation for your partner, both big and small. Share compliments, offer words of encouragement, and actively engage in activities you both enjoy. These small gestures, woven into the fabric of your daily life, strengthen the foundation of love.

Remember, communication is a journey, not a destination.

There will be bumps along the road, moments of misunderstanding and miscommunication. But by embracing these skills with patience and empathy, you can build a language of love that speaks volumes, creating a deeper, more fulfilling connection with your partner.

Bonus Tip: Remember, communication is a two-way street. While this chapter focuses on honing your skills, remember that your partner also plays a crucial role. Encourage open and honest communication from both sides and create a safe space where vulnerability and understanding can thrive With dedication and practice, these skills can help you navigate the ever-evolving landscape of love, ensuring that your relationship continues to blossom with every shared word and unspokenunderstanding.

Chapter Six: Past Relationships: Healing from Traumas Healing from Past

The Impact of the Past on the Present:

Past emotional experiences, particularly those from previous relationships, can leave lasting scars that result in feelings of despair or lack of self-confidence. Infidelity, rejection, or maltreatment can have negative repercussions on how a person interacts in their future relationships.

As a result, individuals may adopt defensive mechanisms such as self-isolation or aggressive behavior. These behaviors can significantly impact the quality of one's current relationships.

Healing Strategies for Emotional Wounds:

- *There are several steps one can take to gradually heal from past wounds and recover:*

- *Reflect on and journal daily about the emotional experience from the past.*

- *Listen to yourself with kindness and acceptance.*

Identify the personal growth that emerged from that experience.

Accept the pain without running from it, and slowly confront it.

Engage in open communication with trustworthy friendsor seek professional therapy in complex cases.

Practice hobbies and leisure activities to reduce tension.

Avoid entering new relationships until you achieve inner peace and confidence.

The healing process is lengthy and requires patience and determination. However, the outcome will be a sense of liberation from the painful past.

Understanding the healing process, including seeking professional help and allowing oneself to fully embrace the emotional spectrum, is crucial to reclaiming control over one's emotional and relational well-being. The journey is daring and sometimes entails exploring dark corners, but it is necessary for self-growth, self-respect, and fulfilling relationships.

Recognize that pain and healing are part of life, and the more willingness there is to face the emotional wounds, the closer one gets to recovering. Sexual intimacy, when approached with mindfulness and mutual respect, plays a significant role in the healing process and in forming healthy relationships. Remember, healing is possible, and relief from past pain is within reach.

Embracing Farewell:

Healing After Love's End: Love, with its intoxicating cocktail of joy and vulnerability, leaves an indelible mark on the mind. When

a relationship ends, the imprints remain, leaving us grappling with the echoing absence of a once-familiar presence. Accepting the finality of this chapter while navigating the complex emotions unleashed can feel like traversing an emotional labyrinth.

Understanding the Neurochemical Impact:

Love triggers a cascade of neurochemicals, flooding the brain with dopamine, oxytocin, and serotonin, creating feelings of euphoria, attachment, and contentment. When the relationship dissolves, these chemicals plummet, leading to withdrawal symptoms similar to drug dependence. This explains the craving, anxiety, and even physical pain associated with heartbreak.

Navigating the Emotional Maze:

Acknowledge your emotions - denial only prolongs the suffering. Allow yourself to grieve, whether through tears, journaling, or talking to a trusted confidante. Suppressing emotions can hinder healing.

Remember, you are not alone:

Reach out to your support system - friends, family, or a therapist. Sharing your pain in a safe space can lessen the burden and help you gain perspective.

Avoid rebound relationships:

A rebound relationship is a romantic relationship that someone enters shortly after a breakup, often without fully processing the emotions and experiences of the previous relationship. They may be motivated by a variety of factors, such as loneliness, fear of being alone, or a desire to avoid *dealing with their pain.*

Risks of rebound relationships:

Emotional baggage*: Unresolved feelings from the previous relationship can interfere with the new one, making it difficult to form a genuine connection.*

Unrealistic expectations: The new partner may be seen as a replacement for the ex, leading to disappointment and frustration.

Rushed pace*: Rebound relationships often progress quickly, which can skip important steps in healthy relationship development, such as getting to know each other and building trust.*

Unfairness to the new partner*: The new partner may be*

unknowingly drawn into a situation where they are not getting their emotional needs met.

Alternatives to rebound relationships:

Focus on healing: Allow yourself time to grieve the end of your previous relationship and process your emotions before entering a new one. Build self-esteem: Focus on activities that make you feel good about yourself and develop a strong sense of self-worth. Connect with friends and family: Surround yourself with supportive people who can provide emotional support during this difficult time.

Remember:

It is important to be honest with yourself and your potential partner about your emotional state and motivations for entering a new relationship. If you are concerned that you may be in a rebound relationship, it is helpful to talk to a therapist or counselor who can provide guidance and support.

Reprogramming Your Mind:

Practice self-care: Prioritize healthy habits like nutritious meals, exercise, and sleep. Engage in activities you enjoy, rediscovering passions put aside during the relationship.

Mindfulness and meditation:

These practices help soothe the emotional storm and foster self-compassion. They allow you to observe your thoughts and feelings without judgment, gradually detaching from negative patterns.

Reframe your narrative:

Instead of dwelling on the "what-ifs," focus on the lessons learned and personal growth fostered by the relationship. View the ending as an opportunity for self-discovery and positive change.

Embrace self-love:

This journey is about rediscovering and nurturing your own worth. Engage in activities that make you feel good about yourself, whether it's learning a new skill, spending time in nature, or simply appreciating your own company.

healing is not linear:

There will be good days and bad days. Be patient with yourself and celebrate your progress, no matter how small.

Love's Legacy:

While the relationship may have ended, the lessons learned and personal growth fostered remain. Carry the positive aspects forward, allowing them to enrich your future endeavors.

Remember, love, even in its impermanence, is a testament to your capacity for connection and vulnerability. As you heal, embrace the open road ahead, knowing that your journey of love and self-discovery continues.

Additional Tips:

- *Consider limiting contact with your ex, especially in the early stages of healing.*

- *Engage in activities that promote personal growth and self-discovery.*

- *Seek professional help if you struggle to cope with the emotional burden.*

Remember, healing takes time and self-compassion. Be gentle with yourself, celebrate your progress, and embrace the exciting possibilities that lie ahead. As you weather the storm and rebuild your life, remember that love's legacy, the strength you gained, and the lessons learned will forever be a part of who you are.

Chapter Seven: Building
ealthy Relationships Appling
What You've Learned

Now that you've explored yourself and learned communication skills and healing from the past, you're in the best position to build positive relationships. In this chapter, we will discuss some fundamental elements to consider when nurturing and growing a relationship:

Mutual Respect:

Mutual respect entails respecting each other's opinions, feelings, and personal boundaries, never allowing narcissism or control to tarnish the relationship. It also comprises listening to each other, acknowledging each other's efforts, and respecting each other's building blocks. This is a foundation for building any healthy relationship.

Open Communication:

This means absolute transparency devoid of hiding any information or emotions. Moreover, it entails earlydetection and prompt communication of any issues that arise. Additionally, expressing needs, goals, and sensual constructive feedback strengthens the bond between you.

Conflict Resolution:

Disagreements are inevitable sometimes, but the key is managing and responding to them healthily. Both parties must listen to one another and focus on resolving the issueat hand rather than dwelling on mistakes.

Furthermore, maintain constructive language during a conversation.

To construct a healthy relationship based on trust and respect, put in the effort to build these elements every day. Now, let's dive deeper into the aspect of conflict resolution. To maintain a healthy relationship, keep in mind the following advice for effectively resolving disputes:

Calm Your Emotions:

When faced with disagreement, avoid reacting impulsively. Instead, take a step back to process the situation, arrange your thoughts, and allow your emotionsto subside.

Listen to What Your Partner Has to Say:

Pay close attention to your partner, striving to truly comprehend their perspective. Put ego aside and open your mind to different ways of thinking.

Identify the Problem:

Identify the precise problem and express it in a non-confrontational manner.

Think About the Solutions Approach the situation with a problem-solving mindset.

Suggest and propose solutions to the issue instead of dwelling on the problem.

Compromise: Consider your partner's perspective andmake concessions when necessary.

Find mutual ground and a resolution that satisfies both parties.

***Mark My Words**: conflict resolution can be an opportunity to strengthen the bond between you and your partner. Introducing vulgar language or personal insults during discussions will only exacerbate the situation and potentially damage the relationship. Regardless of whether you're arguing about monogamy, the division of labor, or finances, apply these five principles to resolve any disagreement effectively. Healthy relationships flourish because of respect, trust, and the ability to resolve conflicts constructively. Put in the effort to strengthen these elements, and watch your relationship grow.*

CHAPTER EIGHT: CONFRONTING
CHALLENGES & CRISES

The Inevitability of Challenges:

Let's face it, challenges and crises are unavoidable in any relationship striving for health. But what truly matters is how we choose to confront them.

Crises often serve as opportunities to test the resilience and strength of a relationship. Challenges may include:

- Disagreements on significant matters such as family or finances.
- Personal or health-related pressures experienced by one partner.
- Family or work-related crises requiring support.
- Temporarily long-distance separations due to job requirements, Long-distance separation that threatens the very fabric of your relationship.
- Screaming matches about the f*cking bills.

Strategies for Confronting Crises:

- *Address issues gradually, avoiding emotional outbursts.*
- *Offer emotional support and sympathy to the injured party.*
- *Accept the other's perspective and seek middle-ground solutions.*
- *Maintain open communication, and share love, and reassurances to overcome the crisis.*
- *Avoid casting blame and share responsibility.*
- *Create a safe space for communication: Choose a calm and private setting to talk, and avoid discussing problems when you're feeling angry or upset.*
- *Practice active listening: Pay close attention to your partner's feelings and try to understand their perspective without interrupting them.*
- *Focus on "I" statements: Instead of blaming your partner, use "I" statements to express how their actions or words affect you. This helps avoid defensiveness and encourages open communication.*
- *identify the root cause of the problem: Don't just focus on the surface-level issue. Try to understand the underlying reasons for the conflict.*

Be willing to compromise: Both partners need to be willing to find a solution that works for everyone involved. Be open to different perspectives and be prepared to make some concessions.

With patience and understanding, together, you can overcome any obstacle. Strong relationships endure the test of time.

Face the Fire Together: Let's cut the crap - challenges and crises are inevitable in any relationship. What truly matters is how strong you are together to endure and rise above them. These tests aren't easy, they might just burn your relationship to the ground. Disagreements and conflicts are inevitable in any relationship, even between lovers. The key to a healthy relationship is learning how to resolve these issues effectively.

*With patience, understanding, a healthy dose of this sh*t," and a willingness to stand by each other, you can overcome any f*cking obstacle. Remember, strong relationships don't just survive, they thrive in the fire.*

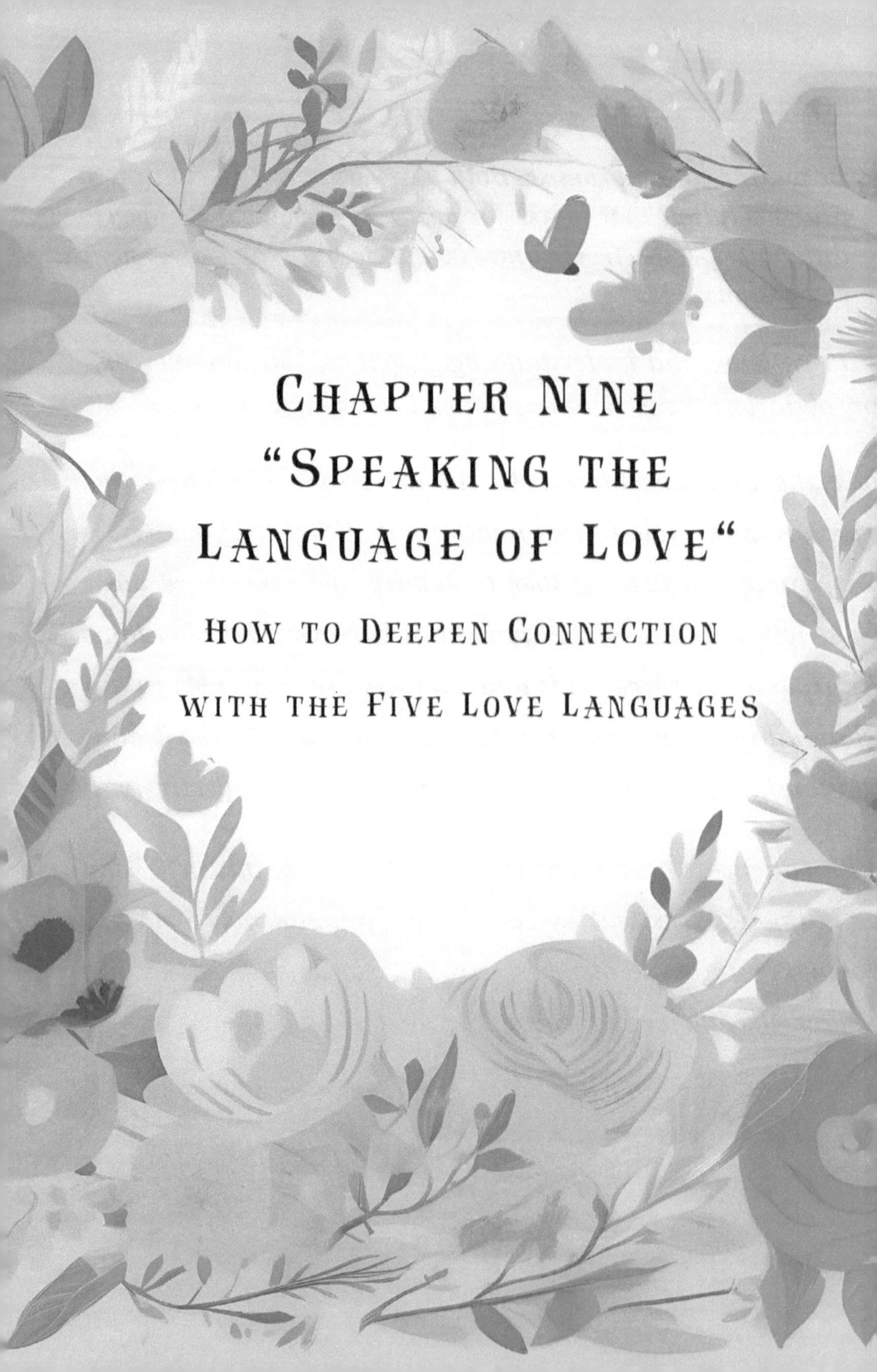

CHAPTER NINE
"SPEAKING THE
LANGUAGE OF LOVE"
HOW TO DEEPEN CONNECTION
WITH THE FIVE LOVE LANGUAGES

Love, that enigmatic force, can feel beautifully complex and frustratingly confusing. One partner craves whispered compliments, while the other thrives on shared adventures. This disconnect doesn't signify incompatibility, but rather, a difference in how love is perceived and expressed. Enter the Five Love Languages, a framework by Gary Chapman that illuminates these varying preferences. By identifying your own and your partner's love language, you unlock a powerful tool to strengthen your connection.

The Five Love Languages:

Words of Affirmation: *These individuals feel loved through verbal expressions of appreciation, compliments, and encouragement. Think genuine praise, handwritten notes, or simply saying "I love you" more often.*

Quality Time: For these individuals, love is about focused, uninterrupted attention. Put away distractions, engage in meaningful conversations, and plan activities you both enjoy. Quality is key, not quantity.

Acts of Service: These individuals feel loved when their partner takes action to lighten their load or make their lives easier. Doing chores, running errands, or remembering small needs showcases love in a tangible way.

Physical Touch: Non-sexual physical affection like hugs, cuddles, or holding hands speaks volumes to these

individuals. Respecting personal boundaries is crucial, but don't underestimate the power of a gentle touch.

Receiving Gifts: This doesn't equate to materialism! It's about the thoughtfulness behind the gift, a symbol of love and recognition. It could be a small token, a homemade creation, or something they genuinely need.

Speaking Your Partner's Language:

Once you identify your partner's love language, tailor your expressions of love accordingly. Here are some examples:
Words of Affirmation: *Leave love notes hidden in unexpected places, write heartfelt poems, or express genuine appreciation for their qualities.*

Quality Time*: Plan a weekend getaway, engage in their favorite hobby together, or simply have deep, attentive conversations without distractions.*

Acts of Service*: Run their errands, cook their favorite meal, or offer to help with a challenging task they're facing.*

Physical Touch: *Offer massages, hold hands during walks, or cuddle while watching a movie. Remember to respect their comfort level and boundaries.*

Receiving Gifts: *Find something thoughtful and personalized, whether it's a book they've mentioned wanting, tickets to an event they'd enjoy, or something handmade that shows you care.*

Take this advice from me, dear reader, Love languages are not static. They can evolve over time, so open communication is key.

Don't neglect your own love language. Ensure your needs are met too. The most important aspect is genuine effort and understanding. Even small gestures, tailored to their language, can speak volumes.

By embracing the Five Love Languages, you unlock adeeper understanding of your partner and yourself. It's a journey ofcontinuous learning and growth, enriching your connection and fostering a love that truly speaks its own language.

Chapter Ten: Culti-vating True Love

Lessons Recap:

Throughout this guide, we explored several key topics to enhance your skills in building warm and sustainable

relationships.

We discussed the importance of self-discovery and self-acceptance.

We learned effective communication techniques

and conflict-resolution strategies. We covered healing from the past, overcoming fears, and insecurities, as well as managing challenges.

These themes emphasized that self-love and self-acceptance are fundamental to establishing lasting relationships. The individual who loves and accepts themselves can freely give and receive love from others with honesty and dedication.

The Journey Continues:

The pursuit of true love doesn't end with finishing this guide. Personal and emotional growth is a continuous journey throughout one's life. As you learn more about yourself and accept yourself, your ability to love and maintain that love grows.

Your journey will face new challenges, so don't lose hope. Keep reviewing and applying the lessons you've learned. And always remember that true love is life's greatest reward. Don't hesitate to put in the effort to achieve it and enjoy it.

Wise Words

"We are all a little weird and life's a little weird. And when we find someone whose weirdness is compatible with ours, we join up with them and fall in mutual weirdness and callit love." - Dr. Seuss

"Nothing can replace love, for love replaces everything." Let love be your goal and driving force on this fantastic journey.

Content :

Crises often serve as opportunities to test the resilience and strength of a relationship in this chapter we learn to do that.

Chapter 9: *Speaking the language of love.............. The difference in how love is perceived and expressed with the Five Love Languages*

Chapter 10: *Cultivating true love ...."Nothing can replace love, for love replaces everything." Let love be your goal and driving force on this fantastic journey.*

References:

Books:
"Insight Meditation" by Joseph Goldstein.
"Radical Self-Love" by Gala Darling, "The Road Less Traveled" by M. Scott Peck.
"Dare to Lead" by Brené Brown, "Feeling Good: The New Mood Therapy"by David D. Burns.
"Nonviolent Communication" by Marshall B. Rosenberg, "How to WinFriends and Influence People" by Dale Carnegie.
"Healing the Shame That Binds You" by John Bradshaw, "Hold Me Tight: Seven Conversations for a Lifetime of Love" by Sue Johnson.
"Attached" by Amir Levine & Rachel S.F. Heller, "The Five Love Languages" by Gary Chapman.
"Man's Search for Meaning" by Viktor Frankl, "The Obstacle Is the Way" by Ryan Holiday.
"Love Sense" by Susan Campbell, "The Seven Principles for Making Marriage Work" by John Gottman & Nan Silver.
"The Five Love Languages" by Gary Chapman.

Websites:
"[www.helpguide.org]"
" [mindful org], [greatergood.berkeley.edu] "."
[psychcentral com], [verywellmind com] ". "
[anxietybc com], [psychologytoday com] ".
" [themighty com], [skillsyouneed com] ".
" [goodtherapy org], [aconsciousrelationship com] ". "
[gottman institute com], [psychology Today com] "."
[apa org], [helpguide org] ".
" [gottman institute com], [verywellmind com] ".

This guide aims to help you overcome the obstacles that may hinder the development of deep and lasting relationships. It will provide you with practical advice and techniques for improving communication skills and self-discovery throughout its chapters. Additionally, you will learn about the leading theories that explain the mechanics of love and relationships.